KIDS CAN COPE

Take Charge of Anger

by Gill Hasson

illustrated by Sarah Jennings

free spirit

PUBLISHING®

Published in North America by Free Spirit Publishing Inc., Minneapolis, Minnesota, 2019

Library of Congress Cataloging-in-Publication Data
Names: Hasson, Gill, author. | Jennings, Sarah, illustrator.
Title: Take charge of anger / written by Gill Hasson ; illustrated by Sarah Jennings.
Description: Minneapolis, Minnesota : Free Spirit Publishing, [2019] | Series: Kids can cope | Audience: Age: 6–9.
Identifiers: LCCN 2018054297 | ISBN 9781631984570 (hardcover) | ISBN 1631984578 (hardcover)
Subjects: LCSH: Anger in children—Juvenile literature.
Classification: LCC BF723.A4 H37 2019 | DDC 155.4/1247—dc23 LC record available at https://lccn.loc.gov/2018054297

Edited by Alison Behnke and Marjorie Lisovskis

Free Spirit Publishing
An Imprint of Teacher Created Materials
6325 Sandburg Road, Suite 100
Minneapolis, MN55442
(612) 338-2068
help4kids@freespirit.com
www.freespirit.com

First published in 2019 by Franklin Watts, a division of Hachette Children's Books · London, UK, and Sydney, Australia

Copyright © The Watts Publishing Group, 2019

The rights of Gill Hasson to be identified as the author and Sarah Jennings as the illustrator of this Work have been asserted in accordance with the Copyright, Designs and Patents Act, 1988.

Series editor: Jackie Hamley

Series designer: Cathryn Gilbert

KIDS CAN COPE

Take Charge of Anger

by Gill Hasson

illustrated by Sarah Jennings

Everybody gets angry—even grown-ups.

But you can find ways to deal with anger and feel better. Really!

This book gives lots of ideas you can use to take charge of anger.

It's no fun to feel angry.

What is anger?

Anger happens when life isn't how you want it to be.
When things go badly or don't seem fair. Or when
you get blamed for something you didn't do.

Maybe you get angry when you don't get what you
want or when people don't keep their promises.

When you're scared or hurt, you might get angry.
You might feel angry if you lose or break something.
Or you may get mad when you don't understand
an idea or can't make something work.

It's not fair!

you promised!

Any of these things can lead to angry thoughts and feelings.

Sometimes your anger might start slowly and get bigger and stronger. You get more and more wound up. Other times, something happens and you feel very angry right away.

Either way, before you know it, your anger can get so big that you lose control. Then you may say or do something that makes everything worse.

I don't want to!

Leave me alone!

I hate you!

I can't make it work!

Is anger bad?

Being angry isn't wrong or bad. Everyone feels angry sometimes. But anger can be a problem when it makes things worse. You might break or damage something, or get into trouble. It is also a problem if your anger hurts or scares you or other people, or if you feel angry a lot of the time.

It is important to learn to deal with your anger so you feel more in control. When you take charge of your feelings, anger can even be useful. It can help you change something that's not right or isn't fair.

I'm angry that you're being so mean. STOP IT!

How do you feel when you're angry?

In cartoons, when someone gets angry, steam comes out of their ears and their eyes bulge. Their body swells up. Maybe their face turns red.

When you're angry, does steam come out of your ears? Probably not!

But you might feel hot. Your heart might start thumping.
Perhaps it feels like your head or body will explode.
What do you do when you feel this way?

Do you jump up and down?
Kick and stomp your feet?
Bang and slam, yell and cry,
scream and shout?
Push, pull, or hit?

Sometimes you might
squash your anger.
Maybe you don't say
or do anything.
You just grit your teeth
and clench your fists.
But you're boiling
mad inside!

When other people don't understand

Sometimes other people don't understand why you're angry or might not listen to you explain what you're angry about.

They might get angry too. Or they might just tell you to "calm down."

They might ignore you or laugh at you. Then you may feel even more angry and annoyed!

Calm down now, please.

It's true that you can't make other people do what you want or make things happen just the way you hope.

And you can't always make things fair or right. But there are things you can do! You can learn ways to take charge of your anger and feel better.

Anger warning signs

Think of a time when you were angry. What angry thoughts did you have? Could you feel your heart pounding or your stomach twisting? Did you want to hit and shout? Did you feel very hot and like you might burst?

These are some anger warning signs.

They are things you start to feel, think, say, and do that let you know you're getting angry. They're like alarms in your mind and body. When an alarm clock rings, it's telling you to wake up and get out of bed. Anger warning signs do the same thing. They tell you that you need to pay attention. You're getting angry!

What do you think your anger warning signs are? How might you deal with your anger?

Slow down and clear your head

When you're angry, your mind fills up with angry thoughts. Then it feels like your brain has no room left for thoughts that could help you.

Anger can happen very fast. But if you can slow things down, your mind can make space for helpful thoughts again.

Then you'll feel more in control. You'll be able to think more clearly. So how can you slow things down?

Press the pause button

Moving away and taking a break from what you're angry about can give you time to calm down, feel better, and think more clearly. Then you can come up with a helpful way to deal with the problem. Moving away and taking a break is like pressing a PAUSE button.

If you can, go somewhere quiet. Somewhere you like to be and where you feel safe.

If you're at home, you could go to your bedroom or to a different room. You could even take a bath or shower.

If you're on the playground, you could play somewhere else for a while.

If you're in the classroom, maybe you could ask your teacher if you could go somewhere safe and quiet.

This isn't always easy. You have to **make** yourself move away and take some time out. Can you think of something you can say or think to yourself that might help you do this? You could try "Stop!" or "Pause!" or "Time out!" or "Step away!" or "Move away!"

Focus on other thoughts

Even if you can't move away from the problem, you can still turn your mind away from angry thoughts. This makes it easier to think calmer, more helpful thoughts.

Here are a few ideas for changing your focus.

Count to four as you breathe in. Then count to four as you breathe out. Each time you breathe out, imagine breathing out all the hot anger.

Do this a few times. Breathing like this can help slow things down and calm your angry thoughts.

Say the alphabet backward.
Or repeat a phrase such as "I can
be calm" or "I can take charge."

I can be calm.

Sing a song in your head until you
feel calmer. Or concentrate on
something you have in front of
you, like a book or toy.

Ali is angry that Isabelle won't let him have his turn on the
computer. To stop his anger from getting out of control, Ali
goes to the other side of the classroom. He breathes out his
anger until he feels calmer and can think of what to do next.

Step away!

Let your anger out

Sometimes you may want to hit and kick or smash and rip to let out your anger. That's when you need to use up your angry energy safely, in a way that doesn't hurt you or anyone else or get you into trouble.

You could stomp your feet when you're feeling mad.
Or run very fast.
You might find it helpful to kick or throw a ball.
Or skip or do jumping jacks.

You could also play some music and do an angry dance.

You could squeeze a pillow really hard and tell yourself that you're squeezing out your anger.

Or you might want to just let it all out by crying and feeling upset for a while.

Talk about how you feel

Another way to let off steam and let out your anger is talking to someone about it. You could talk to a parent or another family member. You could talk to a teacher or a friend. Share that you're upset and angry, and ask the person to listen for a few minutes.

If you don't find a person to talk with, you can even tell a pet or a toy how you're feeling.

Telling someone else what you're angry about can help a lot. The person you talk to might have ideas about what you can do about the problem. Your dog, cat, or toy might not be able to help you, but they can still be good listeners! And that can help you feel better too.

If you can't talk to an adult you know and trust—a teacher or someone in your family—you can talk to someone on the phone. Look at page 28 to learn more about this.

I'm so angry! Isabelle said I could have a turn today, but now she says I can't!

Solve the problem

If the problem you're angry about is something you can solve, you can try to sort it out. First you need to think about exactly what the problem is. What started your angry thoughts? Then think about what you want to happen. What do you want to change? What ideas do you have? Can you deal with the problem yourself or do you need some help?

Sofia was angry because her little sister Ella went into the bedroom they share and broke Sofia's model dinosaur.
Sofia told her mom she didn't want Ella to go into their room when she wasn't there. Sofia's mom said that wasn't possible, and asked Sofia to come up with another plan.

Sofia suggested keeping her special things out of Ella's reach instead. Mom thought that was a great idea. Sofia rebuilt the dinosaur and put it on top of the wardrobe, away from Ella.

Make your own plan

What is something you often feel angry about?
Maybe you could make a plan to deal with this problem.

If you can, ask a grown-up or a friend to help you
think about what to do when you get angry.
When you've made your plan, write it down or draw it.

Keep it somewhere you can easily see it to remind you.
You could even practice your plan with someone.
What will you say if the same thing happens again?
What will you change so your anger doesn't take over?

Then if the problem happens again and you start to feel your
anger warning signs, tell yourself, "Stop! I have a plan!"

Let your anger go

Sometimes you'll be able to sort out a problem and make a plan. Other times, you might realize that there's nothing you can do about the problem.

You may even feel like it's not worth getting angry about. You might realize that being angry will only hurt you. Then you might decide to let your anger go.

Letting your anger go means telling yourself there's no point exploding, lashing out, or sulking. It's not worth hurting someone else or making things worse. You can do something positive instead of wasting your time feeling mad and upset.

Letting it go means telling yourself to think of something else and do something else.

Take charge of anger

Now you know that you can do things to take charge of your anger and feel calmer and happier. Here are some reminders:

- Look for your anger warning signs.

- Help yourself think more clearly. You can press the pause button and count, breathe deeply, sing a song, or find something quiet to do.

- Use up your angry energy in a safe way, such as by squeezing a pillow.

- Talk to someone you trust about how you feel.

- Solve the problem if you can, either on your own or with someone else's help.

- Make a plan to help you take charge of your anger.

- If you can't change what you're angry about, or you decide it's not a big deal after all, let it go.

If your anger feels too big to handle, ask a grown-up for help. If you don't feel you can ask anyone you know, you can call **1-800-448-3000**, text **CONNECT** to **741741**, or go to **yourlifeyourvoice.org** to talk with a counselor. This person will listen to you and give you help and advice about what to do if you're angry about something.

Remember, anger is not bad. Everyone feels angry sometimes.

The good news is that now you can recognize your anger warning signs . . .

. . . and take charge of your anger!

Activities

These drawing and writing activities can help you think about how to manage your anger. You could keep your pictures and writing with this book so that you have your own ideas about how to cope when you're feeling angry.

- Look in the mirror and make an angry face. Draw a picture of it.

- Think of a time when you were angry. Did someone say or do something to trigger your angry feelings? How did you feel? What did you say? What did you do? Draw a picture or write a story about what happened.

- What do you think your anger warning signs are? Draw a picture of what happens in your body when you're angry.

- Write a list of things you like doing that can help move your mind away from angry thoughts and make room for more helpful thoughts.

- Rosa is angry because her mom blamed her for getting chocolate on the sofa. Rosa knows it was really her brother Ben who made the mess. What do you think Rosa could do about it?

- Rafi doesn't understand his math homework. He's getting angry and upset. What ideas do you have for Rafi?

- Write out a plan to deal with something you get angry about. Draw some pictures of yourself in each part of your plan.

- Which of these problems would you try to solve? Which of them would you decide to let go because you can't change them or because they're not a big deal after all?
  - Your dad is telling you to hurry up but you can't find your coat.
  - Your friend can't come over for a sleepover because her mom says she's not allowed.
  - Your brother keeps teasing you and calling you a baby.
  - You find a hole in your favorite shirt.
  - Your friends won't let you join the game they're playing.

Notes for teachers, parents, and other adults

Missing out or being excluded, being unfairly blamed for something, or feeling anxious or scared—these are just a few of the reasons why children may get angry. It's okay to be angry and to want to put right something that's wrong or unfair. It's not easy though, to know what to do with the strong feelings that come with anger and how to avoid making things worse.

When children are angry—just like when adults get angry—they can be unreasonable and illogical. The anger has taken over the rational mind, and the ability to think in a calm, reasonable way has been temporarily switched off. Children need effective techniques and strategies to help them calm down and take control. *Take Charge of Anger* explores ways children can learn to manage their anger.

Although children can read this book by themselves, it will be more helpful for both of you to read it together. Talk with children about the sort of things that trigger their angry feelings.

Help children spot their anger warning signs, and if *you* see the early signs of anger in a child, say so. These warning signs are cues telling children that they can try strategies to manage their anger. You can help children use a range of strategies to calm down and gain control: making a plan to deal with their anger, coming up with ideas for using angry energy safely, and finding ways to turn their mind away from angry thoughts.

Some children might want to read this book all at once. Others will find it easier to manage and understand a few pages at a time. Either way, you'll find plenty to talk about with children. For example, discuss the characters in the illustrations. Ask your child questions such as: "Do you ever feel like that?" "What do you think of that idea?" "How could that work for you?"

Taking some time to think about how things have worked out after an angry episode helps children learn about themselves and what does and doesn't work for them. Praise children's honest efforts, no matter how small. This will build children's confidence that they can do things to help them cope and manage their anger. If something didn't turn out so well, talk together about what they could have done differently.

After reading the book and helping children identify strategies that could work for them, you can come back to the book often to remind yourselves of ideas and suggestions for managing anger. With time, patience, support, and encouragement from you, children will learn to manage their anger better. However, if you're concerned that their anger is frequently causing them to get out of control and is harmful to them or others, it's worth seeking more advice. Reach out to a healthcare provider, counselor, or other expert and ask for help.